Our Bodies

Our Bones

Charlotte Guillain

Heinemann Library
Chicago, Illinois

www.heinemannraintree.com
Visit our website to find out
more information about
Heinemann-Raintree books.

To order:

☎ Phone 888-454-2279

💻 Visit www.heinemannraintree.com
to browse our catalog and order online.

Editorial: Rebecca Rissman, Laura Knowles, Nancy Dickmann,
  and Sian Smith
Picture research: Ruth Blair and Mica Brancic
Designed by Joanna Hinton-Malivoire
Original Illustrations © Capstone Global Library Ltd. 2010
Illustrated by Tony Wilson
Printed and bound by Leo Paper Group

14 13 12
10 9 8 7 6 5 4 3 2

Library of Congress Cataloging-in-Publication Data
Guillain, Charlotte.
  Our bones / Charlotte Guillain.
     p. cm. -- (Our bodies)
  Includes bibliographical references and index.
  ISBN 978-1-4329-3596-2 (hc) -- ISBN 978-1-4329-3605-1 (pb) 1.
Bones--Juvenile literature. I. Title.
  QP88.2.G85 2010
  612.7′5--dc22
                      2009022300

Acknowledgments
The author and publisher are grateful to the following for
permission to reproduce copyright material:
Alamy pp.**4**, **22** (© JUPITERIMAGES/ BananaStock); © Capstone Global
Library pp.**8**, **10** (Karon Dubke); Corbis pp.**11** (© Solus-Veer), **14** (©
Morgan David de Lossy), **20** (© MM Productions); iStockphoto p.**16**
(© Christopher Pattberg); Photolibrary pp.**13**, **5** (© Aflo Foto Agency),
15 (Onoky), **17**, **23** (© Phototake Science), **19** (© MedicImage
Limited RF), **21** (© BSIP Medical); Science Photo Library p.**18**
(PASIEKA); Shutterstock p.**9** (© Cindy Minear).

Front cover photograph of sisters doing cartwheels reproduced
with permission of iStockphoto (©2008 Nancy Louie). Back cover
photograph reproduced with permission of Photolibrary (Onoky/ P
Broze).

Every effort has been made to contact copyright holders of any
material reproduced in this book. Any omissions will be rectified in
subsequent printings if notice is given to the publisher.

Contents

Body Parts

Our bodies have many parts.

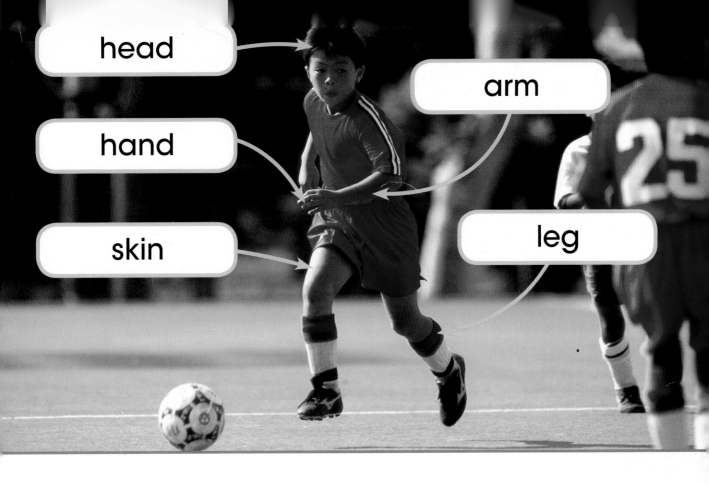

head

arm

hand

skin

leg

Our bodies have parts on
the outside.

5

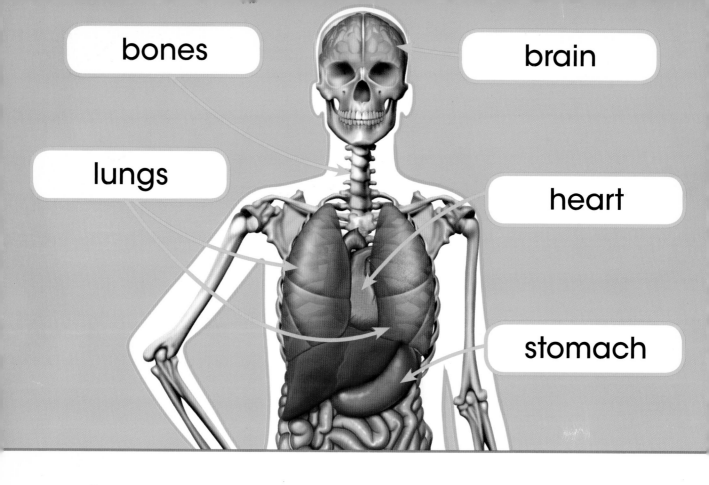

bones

brain

lungs

heart

stomach

Our bodies have parts on
the inside.

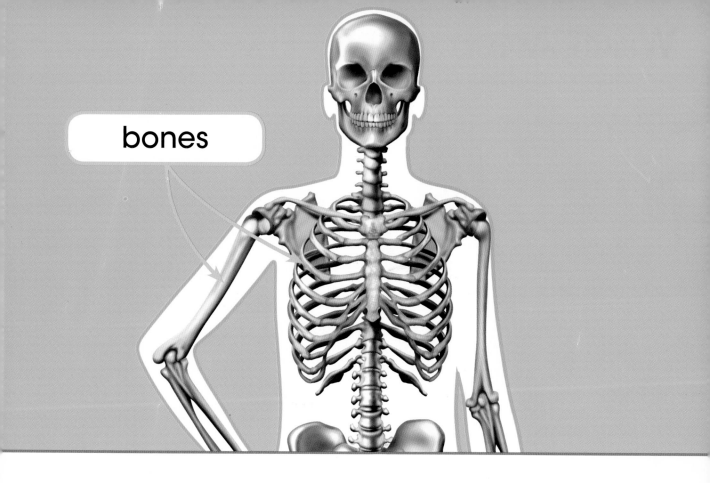

bones

Your bones are inside your body.

Your Bones

You cannot see your bones.

Your bones are in all parts of
your body.

You can feel some of your bones.

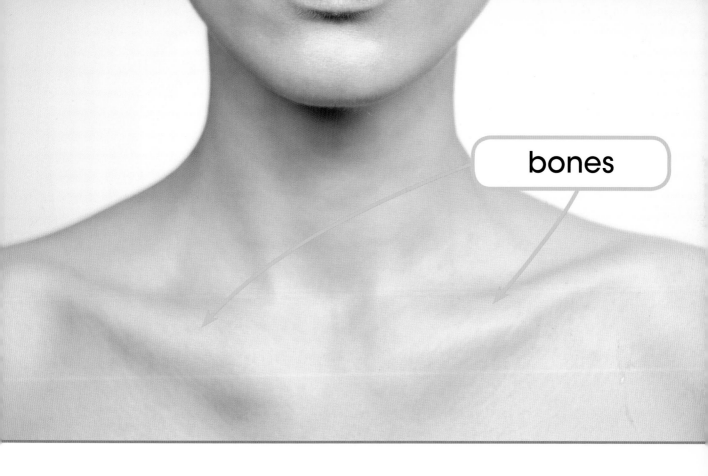

bones

You can see the shape of
some bones.

Your Skeleton

skeleton

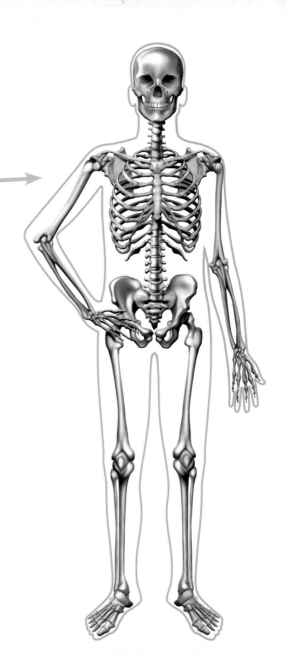

Your bones make up your skeleton.

Your skeleton holds your body up.

Your bones are hard and strong.

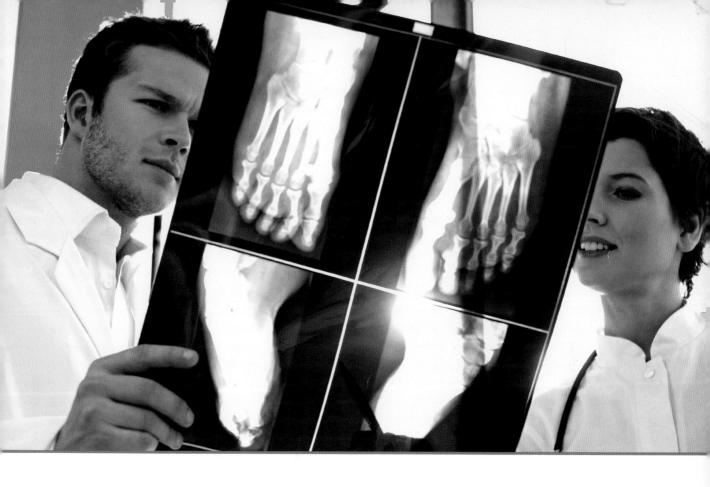

You can see your bones in an
X-ray photo.

What Do Bones Look Like?

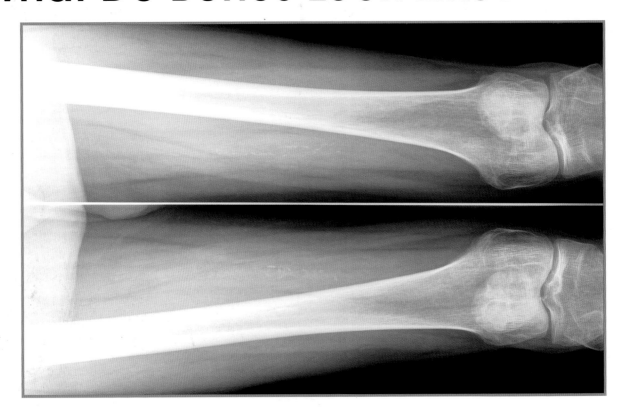

Some bones are long.

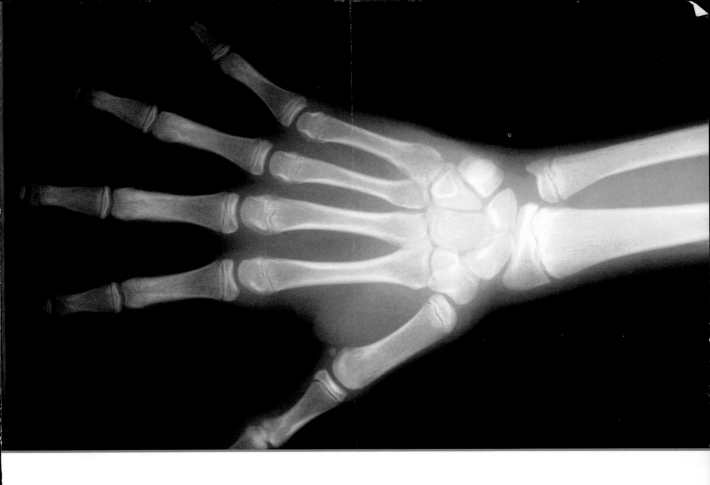

Some bones are small.

What Do Bones Do?

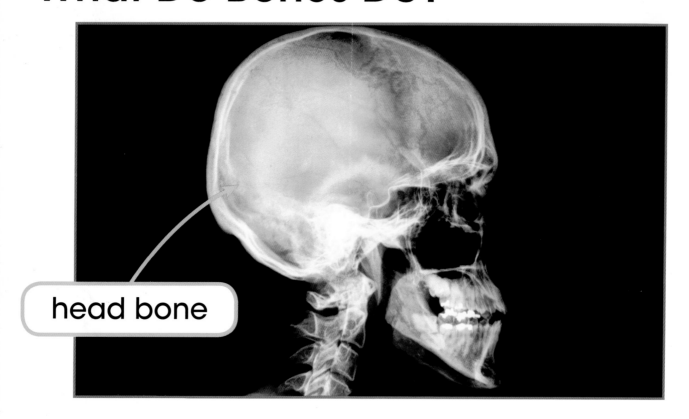

head bone

Bones in your head keep your brain safe.

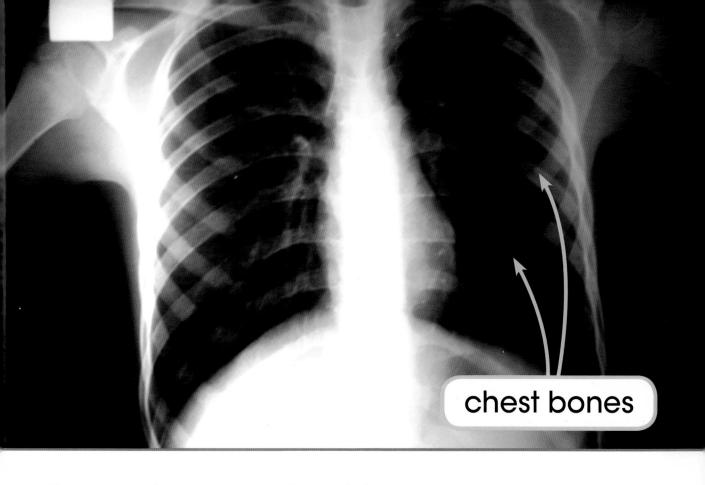

chest bones

Bones in your chest keep your lungs safe.

Staying Healthy

You can exercise to help
your bones.

You can drink milk to help
your bones.

Quiz

Where in your body are your bones?

Answer on page 24

Picture Glossary

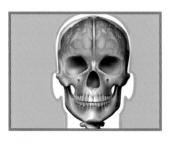 **brain** soft part of your body inside your head. You think with your brain.

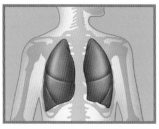 **lungs** two soft parts of your body inside your chest. You use your lungs when you breathe.

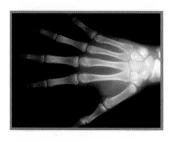 **skeleton** all the bones under your skin that hold your body up

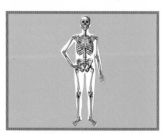 **X-ray** photograph that shows what the bones under your skin look like

23

Index

Answer to quiz on page 22:
Your bones are inside your body.

Notes to parents and teachers
Before reading
Ask children to name the parts of their body they can see on the outside. Then ask them what parts of their body are inside. Make a list of them together and see if the children know what each body part does, for example, stomachs break down food. Discuss where their bones are and see if anyone knows what bones do.

After reading
• Show children a picture of a human skeleton. Ask them how many bones are in their arm (not including their hand). Look together at how bones can be different shapes and sizes.
• Compare the human skeleton with pictures of different animal skeletons. How are they similar? How are they different?
• Ask children if any of them have ever broken a bone. If anyone has, ask him or her to share with the class what happened at the hospital to fix the bone.